DANGEROUS PRAYERS-POWER THROUGH THE PSALMS

And they shall put my NAME upon the children of Israel:
AND I will BLESS THEM (Num 6:27)

Apostle Dennis Adjei-Sarpong

TO GOD BE THE GLORY

DEDICATIONS

This Book is Dedicated to Apostle Eric Kingsley Darko(Founder and Leader of Ancient of Ancients God Ministry, Adabraka, Ghana). He is my father and spiritual mentor under whose wings the LORD took me up. God bless you and increase your anointing.

Hannah Darko –The love of a mother, a true prophetess for the kingdom of God-She gave me both physical and spiritual nourishment.

Ancient of Ancients Prayer Warriors Ministry- Where it all began-Holy ghost fireeeee: Our God is a consuming fire

Prophetess Angela Adjei-Sarpong-my beautiful wife and a great inspiration.

THE TWINS- The Promise of God

Table of Contents

SECTIONS

Foreword

And he spake a parable unto them to this end that men ought always to pray, and not faint...Luke 18:1

From this we realized that prayer is the foundation, central and core pillar of Christianity that triggers all the exploits of the miraculous believer. In buttressing this point, we realize that the master's disciples' according to the eleventh chapter of Luke said Lord teach us how to pray as ....The disciples had walked with Jesus and had seen him working miracles, doing greater works, teaching and preaching, prophesying and healing yet they requested not any of these things but said Lord ''teach us how to pray..''.This is to say that, they caught the revelation secret of the master as getting things done in his ministry was how he could attract the attention of heaven through PRAYER.

I still do not understand why the disciples' did not say Lord pray for us or Lord pray with us but Lord teach us. This means everyone can pray but everyone cannot receive answers to their prayer because heaven's marking scheme may not permit answers to some prayers. Prayer is a secret and a mystery of definition psalm 91:1.

Some people pray few words and they are justified, others pray all their hours and words out and they are frustrated and give up with even increase in their problems.

In this book, Pastor Dennis has outlined perfectly a means and a way to touch the heart of God and move the hand of God through effective and fervent prayers that rents heavens open.

This book by this gifted man of God will not only teach you how to pray but will stir up revival fire of the Lord to lay believers in tracks and in several dimensions of prayer. It will also keep believers awake to their Gods given calling and gifting.

It may interest you, dear reader that I was born into and raised in one of the hardest background but prayer in the right direction and target taught by Pastor Dennis has turned my captivity around. May God turn yours around as you read this book in Jesus' name. Amen. This book is a must have and a must read.

I feel honored to have such a wonderful and God fearing man of God.

PASTOR PETER ADJEI

ANCIENT OF ANCIENTS GOD MINISTRY INT.

Preface

This book was developed as a result of my earnest search of the power of GOD through His Holy Name. Guided by the Holy Spirit I received the mysteries of His Name which enabled me to develop a series of prayers using the Holy Names of God and the power of His word through the Psalms.These prayers have worked miracles in my own personal life and the lives of others who have sought the Lord through this wonderful book. I encourage you to use this book prayerfully and you will see the glory of the Almighty God and His power.

Introduction

The purpose of this book is unlock the mystery surrounding the Holy Names of God and how to prayerfully use them to successfully receive answers to prayers. The prayers contained herein have been consecrated and dedicated in the realms of the Spirit to cause a shift in the heavenly atmosphere. The mystery in the Holy word of God especially the book of psalms is also revealed. The book of psalms have the power of God to change every situation in our life. If you can pray a psalm daily, you will see the tremendous benefits that you will receive as a prayer warrior and how miracles will be released in your life.

Paul, the Apostle said we are not here to give to unto you the enticing words of man's wisdom but of power and demonstration of the Holy Ghost, likewise I challenge you as a man of God not called of men by the Almighty God that if you desire anything in faith and with perseverance and prayer, GOD WILL ANSWER YOUR PRAYERS THROUGH THIS SACRED BOOK. GOD BLESS YOU. WAITING FOR YOUR TESTIMOMY AND MIRACLE IN JESUS NAME

SECTION ONE

Arise, Get up AND FIGHT, this is what I hear the spirit of the Lord say. The challenges of life are sometimes overwhelming but God is saying to us until we contend in a battle through Fervent Prayers, we're not going nowhere. I am here asking questions about certain situations and problems that I face in my life and the more I think about it, the more fear grips me, the more I think about it the more my faith weakens but thank God for the Holy spirit that quickens our mortal bodies to remind us of the strategies to be victorious in life. Are there anybody in here that is going through affliction, problems and circumstances? Beloved God has challenged us to **Arise and Fight**, for He will be with us and has given us the power through prayers to be conquerors. In the book of Luke 10:18-19 - it is written: And JESUS said unto them, I beheld Satan as lightening fall from heaven. Behold I give unto you POWER to tread on serpents and scorpions and over all the power of the enemy: and nothing shall by any means hurt you. Thank JESUS for this power and the mandate through his Blood that washed away our sins to inherit the Righteousness of Our God, we are made righteous and therefore it is written our fervent, passionate prayers will avail much. In the book of Exodus 15:16, it is written that fear and dread shall upon them: by the greatness of thine arm they shall be as still as stone: till thy people pass over, which thou has purchased. Beloved the secret here is that if we recognize that we are purchased by the blood of Jesus, then this promise is ours for the taken, our enemies will experience the terror and fear of the Most High God. Are there any covenant blood warriors here, that want to fight till the battle is won because **our LORD IS MAN OF WAR AND THE LORD IS HIS NAME (exodus 15:3).** Arise soldiers of God, let us Pray, Pray and pray until we see results, like Daniel lets us pray till our Angel of blessing is sent. Amen. I decree and summon you to pray like u never did before in Jesus name.

Be excited! For the Holy Spirit is about to reveal mysteries that will empower your prayer life than ever before. You will be drawn to prayer and pray till the mountain moves into the sea. This revelation is for people who are 'crazy' about prayer and daring God to see divine manifestation in their life.

First to whom do we pray to, as a Christian and a believer, it is imperative to know the power that back our prayer that causes divine manifestation in our life. The Spirit of God Himself is center of our effective prayer. The Almighty God, the creator of the Heavens and Earth is the one Whom we Pray to, and we pray by invoking His name because in His name is His Spirit and Nature. Our name and nature are synonymous and inseparable; therefore when we **CALL UNTO THE NAME OF GOD**, his nature and attribute are released unto us by His Spirit. The Ancient Spirit, who is the creator of the Universe by whom we Christians are subscribed to, is **JEHOVAH**, who appeared to Moses in a burning bush with an ineffable name so terrible, so powerful and so mysterious that it begins and ends with HIM. He saith to Moses **IAM THAT IAM**. In revealing his mysterious name, **YHWH ("I AM HE WHO IS", "I AM WHO AM" or "I AM WHO I AM"**) Exodus 3:14-15, God says who he is and by what name he is to be called. This divine name is mysterious just as God is mystery. It is at once a name revealed and something like the refusal of a name, and hence it better expresses God as what he is - infinitely above everything that we can understand or say: he is the "hidden God", his name is ineffable, and he is the God who makes himself close to men. The Hebrew equivalent of **YHWH is YOD HE VAU HE**, the four letter name of God known as the **Tetragrammaton**, by whom the creation of the world began with and ends with .This name was so Holy and inaccessible to all except the most chosen prophets of God and by that most wonders were performed by him that carried that name. The name of God was put on the Israelites so as to obtain the blessings of God, according to Numbers 6:27.So therefore the derivation of the name JEHOVAH came as an utterable name in prayer to the Creator. Therefore Yeshua (Which is the Hebrew name of JESUS means **JEHOVAH SAVES OR YOD HE SHIN VAU HE**.

The meaning of the Hebrew Yod He SHin Vau Heh

This Awareness indicates that the name Jesus in Hebrew is spelled Yod He Shin Vau Heh. The name Jehovah is Yod He Vau Heh. The "Shin" added to Jesus represents the Spirit. The Yod He, and Vau Heh, the letters on both side of Shin represents Fire, Air, Water and Earth, and thus, Yod He Shin Vau Heh represents a 5th element (spirit) which is the Divine Spirit.

So JESUS therefore controls all the four elements of creation because he is the Divine Spirit that created the Universe (John 1:10). He is seen in the book of Genesis, the Spirit of God moving on the surface of the waters. He is the essence of creation itself and the Father of all creatures and creation, all spirits- both good (angels) and evil (demons) are subjected unto Him so therefore at the mention of the name JESUS JEHOVAH-All things on earth, heaven, seen or unseen must OBEY HIM, without delay. What an **AUTHORITY WE HAVE IN THE NAME JESUS,** THE ANCIENT SPIRIT that became flesh among us that He may redeem us and give us access to His Name-Through HIS BLOOD. The revelation and the mystery here is that God is Holy so much therefore to invoke His name and His presence, we need to be sanctified and purified by sacrifices of blood according to the Old covenant which gave us limited access to his power save the few chosen prophets of God like Moses and Elijah who had the mandate through the name of GOD to control elements and nature. It is expedient to know through the name of God given unto Moses, he controlled the waters at red sea, controlled nature and nurture. The same Spirit operated through Elijah who controlled fire and water.

Stay right here with me, the blood of JESUS therefore gives us access to all the power that is hidden in the Most Sacred name by which EVERYTHING WAS MADE.BECAUSE HIS NAME IS IAM... YOD HE VAU HE.., simply put IAM THAT WHICH CREATED YOU AND THE UNIVERSE.

It is getting interesting here.Ride with the boat because JESUS IS HERE. Precious Holy spirit I pray that you open the mind and hearts of your people to understand your secrets as it revealed now in JESUS NAME.

Therefore as Christians, we possessed the name of JESUS, therefore the promises of Numbers 6:27 is actively working for us in prayer. SO WE THEREFORE GO TO GOD IN PRAYER TO BE BLESSED.

SO IF THERE IS ANYONE WHO WANTS TO BE BLESSED BY GOD ACCORDING TO HIS PROMISE THEN I CHALLENGE YOU TO ENTER INTO PRAYER WITH HIM.(Amos 3:7) states that the secrets of the Lord are with his prophets. I therefore stand by the mercies of God and as a prophet of God to unveil the secrets of the LORD to you so that HE WILL DO SOMETHING WITH YOU RIGHT NOW, RIGHT HERE IN JESUS NAME.

UNVEILING THE SECRETES OF THE OCCULT

You see, there are so many religions and spirits operating in the world today, all drawing their power from the FATHER of ALL spirits. By divine order GOD has ordained every creation of His to be backed by an angel. There are angels guarding the sun, moon, stars, water and air and many more. So when one invokes the name of God to worship the sun, moon, stars and water, He has violated the law of God to worship idols or gods. According to the commandment of God, he states 'and you shall have no other gods besides me'I AM THE LORD, AND I AM A JEALOUS GOD. The name LORD in Hebrew is ADONAI which is translated as MASTER.It means God controls everything, He is sovereign and He shares his glory with no one.

Prophetically, I am mandated by the Holy Spirit to insert another dangerous prayer here before we go ahead with this divine knowledge. So therefore if we call GOD, our LORD- meaning Master.It means we are invoking his lordship and control over all areas of our life- in our finances, marriage, home, business, spiritual life and everything. Watch this! so by faith if you call LORD JESUS, in Hebrew it is ADONAI YESHUA, you are by the power of the Holy Spirit inviting Jesus to fix that which is messed up in your finances, marriage and every area of your life.

If you're still reading, there is a hunger for God, yes and I release LORD JESUS to come into your life right now and established his perfect will in your life right now. I see Jesus rearranging your destiny right now. It is coming out by fire; it is descending from the throne room of God and yes from now on. Yes I said now you are born again by fire and no foul or demonic spirit dares mess with you because JESUS IS LORD OVER YOUR LIFE.AMEN

I feel fresh fire on you. Let's get together, clap your hands and lift Him up higher for fresh oil in Jesus Name. Catch this revelation! Soldiers of God, covenant blood holders, by the mercies of God I beseech you to PRAY, PRAY.PRAY AND PRAY THROUGH GOD and through his name. (Psalm 44:5- Through thee we will push down our enemies: through thy name will we tread them under that rise up against us (AMEN)

DON'T WORRY

Behold the fowls of the air: for they sow not, neither do they reap, nor gather into barns; yet your heavenly Father feedeth them. Are ye not much better than they?(Mat 6:26-27

THE AUTHORITY IN GOD'S NAME AND VOICE

Verily, Verily, all spirits obey God's voice and the devil knows this.**I SAID THE NAME OF GOD IS ADONAI...MEANING LORD OR MASTER** so get ready for this revelation.It is not only Christians who use the name of God to perform miracles, witches and magicians, sorcerers all use the name of God. Stay here, don't be confused...you are in line..thank God.I thought I lost you for a moment: in the book of Exodus 20:7 it **states Thou shalt not take the name of the LORD thy God in vain; for the LORD will not hold him guiltless that taketh his name in vain**

This means that there are people who have spiritual knowledge Of God but will use it in evil manner for their benefits. That knowledge is given by demons (who were once perfect creatures of God who lived with Him and know His ways).Beloved, the devil knows God more than you because he was closer to Him than you, so in the New Testament, he is described as the angel of light. Because he appears like God but he is not God. The only thing the devil and demons are afraid is the name of GOD-JESUS....MEANING JEHOVAH SAVES OR YOD HE VAU HE (TETRAGRAMMATON).By the name YOD HE VAU HE ADONAI (TETRAGRAMMATON-four lettered name of God: YOD HE VAU HE (YHWH) by which Jehovah and Yahweh evolved), one can compel angels and demons to obey them and do their biddings. So summoning demons and angels through the most potent name of God without the WILL OF God means you have used God's name in vain and the LORD will punish you. The reason the demons and angels are subjected to the sorcerers or conjurers is that their LORD's name have been mentioned and they have no choice but to respond to their Master. People enter covenants with these demons to get their request or desires fulfilled and most often the devil provides to them what they need in the expense of their soul or sacrifice. (Mathew 7-21-23).Please read carefully- in summary it said it is not everyone that says LORD, LORD, WILL ENTER MY KINGDOM BUT HE THAT DOETH THE WILL OF GOD.

Beloved, if sorcerers, magicians, and witches even know the power of the name of our God, why then do we that are bought by the precious blood of JESUS, who needs no covenant with demons for GOD to work miracles in our life suffer bondages and live in failure. I summoned you today by the blood of JESUS to pray the names of God through Jesus Christ for they are powerful in undertaking each request for the **LORD IS IN HIS NAME AND THE LORD IS HIS NAME.**

SECTION 2

REDEMPTIVE NAMES OF GOD (Proverbs 18:10...The name of the LORD IS......

JEHOVAH ADONAI-Our Sovereign (Gen 15:2-8)

JEHOVAH ROHI- My shepherd (Psalm 23:1)

JEHOVAH JIREH- The Great Provider (Gen 22:8-14)

JEHOVAH ELOHIM- Our Eternal Creator (Gen 2:4-25)

JEHOVAH TSIDEKENU- Our Righteousness (Jer 23-6)

JEHOVAH EL-SHADDAI- Our Sufficiency-Almighty (Gen 17:1-2)

JEHOVAH SABAOTH- LORD OF HOST (1st Sam 1:3)

JEHOVAH NISSI- Our Banner (Exodus 17:15)

JEHOVAH RAPHA- OUR healer (Ex 15:26)

JEHOVAH –MEKADDISHKEM- Our Sanctifier (Ex 31:13)

JESUS CHRIST- YESHUA H'AMASHIAC-JEHOVAH SAVES-AND HE IS ANOINTED -most potent name against demonic attack—and everything thereof (Philippians 2:10

OTHER NAMES OF GOD ASSIGNED TO PEOPLE

THIS IS A COMFIRMATION OF NUMBERS 6:27-AND THEY SHALL PUT MY NAME UPON THE CHILDREN OF ISRAEL: AND I WILL BLESS THEM

El –bethel – The God of Bethel

El- Elohe Israel, God the God of Israel

Elhanan-grace or mercy of God

Elijah- God the Lord, the strong God

Elishah- It is God, the Lamb of God that giveth help

Gaddiel- the Lord my Happiness

Raphael- the medicine of God

Semachiah- joined to the Lord

Shachia- the protection of the Lord

Samuel- the Lord has heard

POWER IN THE NAME OF JESUS CHRIST

The name of God have so much power that it is the essence of life itself and creation exists because God's name hold it in place. The Bible clearly states that God created the universe with the spoken word and the spoken word according to John 1:1 is the word of God which became flesh and dwelt among us and through that word everything in this world was created. The WORD OF GOD IS THEREFORE JESUS CHRIST MANIFESTED IN THE FLESH. THE NAME JESUS CHRIST in Hebrew is transliterated as Yeshua Hamashiac-which means God saves.This confirms the purpose of which Jesus came into this world to save mankind from sin and from the bondage of the devil.

As a practical apostle of God specialized in deliverance and healing, I have used the name of Jesus Christ to cast out numerous demons and devils and have witness with my own eyes and ears how these demons tremble under the authority of the Holy Ghost in the name of Jesus. According to the scriptures in Mathew 10:1- Jesus called the twelve disciples and gave them power against unclean spirits to cast them out and to heal all manner of sickness and disease. By this authority , the believer can be able in faith cast out demons and heal the sick .The scriptures confirms that at the mention of the name of Jesus every knee should bow and every tongue will confess that Jesus Christ is LORD(Phil 2:10-11).

This affirmation sheds light on the name of GOD which is ADONAI- which is translated LORD OR MASTER- the ONE THAT HAS AUTHORITY-. So by calling on the Holy name of God, we are indeed calling upon Jesus Christ who is the LORD AND MASTER OF THE UNIVERSE, THE CREATOR, THE ALL POWERFUL ONE, WHO HAVE THE POWER TO DEFEAT *satan and his demons.*

SECTION 3

WELCOME TO ABODE OF DANGEROUS PRAYERS:
ONLY FOR THE PRAYER WARRIOR

Spiritual prayers Against Demons

In the name of JESUS CHRIST, by the power of the holy trinity, God the FATHER, God the SON, God the HOLY SPIRIT.I imposed upon you the most high commandment of God, by the omnipotence of the Ever-living God (El- Olam Chai, by the virtue of the Holy GOD and power of Him who spake and all things were made, even by his holy commandments the heavens and earth were made. With all that is in them. I Adjure and compel you , thou foul spirit that torments me by the blood of JESUS CHRIST whose blood thou can't resist, I compel and expel you by the holy ghost whose fire consumeth thee. I compel and cast you out by the most potent name of YESHUA H'AMASHIAC (Jesus Christ) by which you run without delay. I subject you to the terror of God if thou refuses to come out .I subject you to the judgment of GOD now and forever and cast you to pit of hell till the second coming of our LORD AND SAVIOR JESUS CHRIST. Amen.

PRAYER FOR URGENT REQUEST

In the name of JESUS CHRIST OF NAZARETH, I stand in the mercies of God to receive that which belongs to me according to the covenant of the blood of Jesus Christ hear me thou creator of the Universe, Spirit Divine, by the strength of God (Elohim, by the greatness of God, by the unity God, by the most Holy name EHIEEH(IAM) which is the root, trunk, source and origin of all divine names , whence they all draw life and virtue which Adam having invoked he acquired knowledge of all created beings. By the holy words of my savior: Ask and it shall be given to you, I therefore ask that my request (name request) be established to me according to thy holy will, knock and it shall be open, I open all doors of my life according to your holy will, seek and I shall find, I hereby locate my destiny with the light of GOD through JESUS CHRIST MY LORD. Amen.

PRAYER AGAINST DANGEROUS ENEMIES

HEAR me O Great Shepherd of Israel thou that led Joseph like a flock, o thou that are enthroned by the cherubim and seraphim. Most terrible God, in the name of JESUS CHRIST, I Overthrow all my enemies from the four corners of the earth by the blood of JESUS. It is written the ADONAI(THE LORD) IS a man of war , the LORD IS HIS NAME.I hereby destroy all my enemies and them that hate me by the potent name of ADONAI WHICH means LORD, I surrender all my enemies and them that persecute me to the rulership and lordship of JESUS, By the chariots of fire, the flames of fire,, the pillar of fire, fire of Paracletos(comforter), I rain terror and fire over my enemies that they be as stone still now and forever more. By the name of the most potent name EL ADONAI TSABAOTH, which IS GOD LORD OF HOST, by which Joseph invoked and was found worthy to escape from the hands of his brethren, I command my soul to escape all traps of the evil one now and forevermore in JESUS NAME.

PRAYERS AGAINST ILLNESS / DISEASES

In the name of JESUS, hear thou my voice you spirit of sickness and disease, I command thee by the blood of JESUS to leave my body and the body of…….. I compel you by the Holy trinity, by the sign of the cross, by the most precious blood and water that flowed from the side of Jesus, by the sweat which issued from his body when he said in the Garden of Olives: My father if it be thy will let this cup pass from me', by his death and passion, by his burial and glorious resurrection, by his ascension. I command you therefore by the crown of thorns which was set upon his head, by the blood which flowed form his feet and hands, by the nails with which He was nailed to the tree of the cross. I received total healing and command every disorder in my body to be ordered in Jesus NAME.

PRAYER TO BREAK DEMONIC COVENANT

JESUS , JESUS, JESUS, FLAMES OF FIRE, CONSUMING FIRE OF THE MOST HIGH GOD, MOST terrible God in the ineffable name , TETRAGRAMATON..YOD HE VAU HE ,JEHOVAH which being heard the elements are overthrown, the air is shaken, the sea runneth back, the fire is quenched, the earth trembles, and all the host of celestials and terrestrials, and infernal do tremble together and are troubled and confounded. I severe and break any ancestral linkage, marital linkage and demonic covenant either willfully or unwillfully by the blood of JESUS CHRIST, GOD IN THE FLESH ,SEEN OF ANGELS AND OF MEN.Holy Ghost fire descend upon me and purge me through fire by the unquenchable fire at the feet of the most High God. Holy angels, holy chariots, by the name of the Highest, EEL ELYON AND YESHUA, I beseech thee to surround me now and forever more in JESUS NAME.

PRAYER TO RELEASE FINANCIAL BLESSINGS

In the name of JESUS CHRIST, by you all things were created, WORD OF GOD, WORD BECOME FLESH, VOICE OF THE LORD THAT DIVIDE THE FLAMES OF FIRE, by you all things were created and for you. I create my destiny according TO YOUR RICHES AND GLORY. In the name of Jehovah Jireh, thou Great PROVIDER, provide for me now and forever more.EL –Shaddai- Almighty and Sufficient God, I have returned to you now, let me be built up. Let me lay gold as dust.El-shaddai – I receive your blessings to become rich in Jesus name. In the name of the living God. EL- CHAI, through the virtue of alliance with us, by your living power through the blood of EMMANUEL, MESSIAHS, YESHUA H'AMASHIAC, let my finances be brought back to life now and forever more. Thou eternal God, EL OLAM, let not poverty come near me now and forever more. I declare the heavens open by the name of GOD, ELOHIM TSABAOTH, He that ruleth the heavens, let my heavens rain treasure and glory in the name of JESUS CHRIST. Amen.

PRAYER FOR FAVOR BEFORE ALL MEN

I hereby stand in the blood of JESUS, the Great and merciful God, let me be washed with thy blood, thy merciful blood which was shed on the cross for my sake

With my tongue as a sword of God, I cut through all limitations, boundaries and release these words upon my life that through faith in Christ Jesus, everything and everyone will grant me favor without delay. By the judgment of the living and the dead, by the gospel words of Our Savior Jesus Christ, by his preaching, by his sayings, by all his miracles, by the child in swaddling clothes, by the crying child borne by the mother in her most pure and virginal wombs. I Release the angel of favor to be by my side now and forever more in the name of JESUS.

PRAYER FOR PEACE AMONG FRIENDS /FAMILIES

Thou Great Jehovah, Prince of Peace, everlasting Father, Hear me now by the blood of Jesus Christ to grant me peace, tranquility, love and kindness.El Shalom- God of PEACE, Master Jesus, merciful LORD, open thou my heart and let the rivers of peace and love flow within me and my family (mention name) and friends (mention name). Make us lovable, inseparable, bind us together by thy everlasting chords. Spirit of God, Yeshua, Yeshua, Yeshua, the name that Giveth peace, through you let your angel of love and peace descend now in the name of Adonai Elohim Tsabaoth, to dwell with me, to dwell with us now and forever more.Amen

PRAYER AGAINST SEED OF BARENESS

In the name of Yeshua, by the blood of Jesus Christ, by the power of the Holy ghost, I command every seed of bareness to catch fire in Jesus name.Hear the voice of the LORD, you spirit of bareness the word of God is against you, for it is written I will be fruitful and multiply, the God of Abraham, Isaac and Jacob touch my womb now in Jesus MIGHTY NAME.Adonai Elohim Jah by the holy names of GOD..i have conceived , by His authority I am fruitful.

After this prayer read psalm 113 aloud and give God praise. Repeat this prayer for seven days at midnight and anoint your womb with holy anointing oil after reading this prayer. Your miracle baby is on the way. Amen

SECTION 4

**POWER THROUGH THE PSALMS: KING DAVID'S WAY
INTO THE HEART OF GOD**

King David playing His Harp
http://deeptruths.com/letters/images/king-david.jpg

THE PRAYER

Father in the name of Jesus, I pray that you will release your divine counsel that these prayer formula will be embedded in your power and as your beloved servant David prayed to you through the psalms of the Spirit that you heard his voice and cry and turned away his problems . David was a man after your own Heart so we pray that whoever prays these psalms with Faith and a holy Heart, YOU WILL HEAR FROM HEAVEN AND COMMAND YOUR HOLY ANGELS TO FULFIL THE DESIRES OF THEIR HEART IN JESUS MIGHTY NAME.

INTRODUCTION TO THE PSALMS

The Bible is the written word of God, it was written by holy men of God through the power of the Holy Spirit as they had encounters with God through their walk in life. It is a compilation of history, wonders, nature of God, instructions, wisdom, laws and commandment. It is simple the guide to life for mankind. No book has ever been written that holds so much power and authority than the Bible, it is the final authority of a Christian and a believer, through which the believer can achieve their heart's desire by believing and following the words of God. The book of Joshua instructs us that we should meditate upon the word of God daily and do not turn from left or right and be careful to do whatever that is written in , then we can make our way prosperous(Joshua 1:8).

It is with this regard that I introduce to you the Book of Psalms. The book of psalms contains prayers, songs for every occasion in a man's life. It is a complete instruction and spiritual direction and a powerful prayer weapon for the believer. When one prays the psalms wholeheartedly and in faith, miracles are obtained, deliverance takes place, healing is released, spiritual protection is established.

My passion for the psalms began when I was a child and whenever my Dad would prophesy to people, after the prophecy the Holy Spirit would add a psalm to be given to the person to pray alongside the prophecy. Many people were testifying in the church about how their prophecies have been fulfilled. One day I also received a prophecy when I was 14 years of age that I will travel to the United States of America to continue my education and immediately after the prophetic word, a psalm was given to me to pray alongside the prophecy. I believed the prophecy and prayed the psalm that was given to me. God opened the door for me to come to America in 2004 to pursue my education. I was able to go to school and graduate. THE PROPHECY HAS BEEN FULFILED.

The fulfillment of the prophecy was a result of the prayers that I prayed to God using His word the psalms. Ever since God has performed so many miracles in my life and in the lives of others just by simply praying with the psalms and in faith. Through the psalms God has caused His protection and favor to be released in my life and I still continue to pray and use the psalms to pray for people to receive the breakthroughs in life.

Believe God and His word and be part of this prayer mystery and your life will never ever be the same. I am a living testimony to what God can do through the power of the psalms.

The Bible states that whenever Saul was in distress, an evil spirit from the Lord tormented him; David was sent to play the harp- the secret chord of psalms that pleased the Lord and Saul was relieved.

1 Samuel 16:14-23 King James Version (KJV)

[14] But the Spirit of the LORD departed from Saul, and an evil spirit from the LORD troubled him.

[15] And Saul's servants said unto him, Behold now, an evil spirit from God troubleth thee.

¹⁶ Let our lord now command thy servants, which are before thee, to seek out a man, who is a cunning player on an harp: and it shall come to pass, when the evil spirit from God is upon thee, that he shall play with his hand, and thou shalt be well.

¹⁷ And Saul said unto his servants, provide me now a man that can play well, and bring him to me.

¹⁸ Then answered one of the servants, and said, Behold, I have seen a son of Jesse the Bethlehemite, that is cunning in playing, and a mighty valiant man, and a man of war, and prudent in matters, and a comely person, and the LORD is with him.

¹⁹ Wherefore Saul sent messengers unto Jesse, and said, Send me David thy son, which is with the sheep.

²⁰ And Jesse took an ass laden with bread, and a bottle of wine, and a kid, and sent them by David his son unto Saul.

²¹ And David came to Saul, and stood before him: and he loved him greatly; and he became his armourbearer.

²² And Saul sent to Jesse, saying, Let David, I pray thee, stand before me; for he hath found favour in my sight.

²³ And it came to pass, when the evil spirit from God was upon Saul, that David took an harp, and played with his hand: so Saul was refreshed, and was well, and the evil spirit departed from him.

David's calling began when he spent time in prayers with his psalms where his spirit was united with the spirit of God to produce a miracle .When you develop a daily prayer with the book of psalms you will experience the extraordinary breakthroughs and victories that David received.

I hereby declare by the oracles of God and the power therein that your life is been transformed into a faith –living atmosphere and by the sword of the Spirit which is the word of God that you will over-come the trials and hurdles of life in Jesus name.

SPIRITUAL DIRECTION/COUNSEL FOR SPECIFIC LIFE PROBLEMS

The Bible declares in Proverbs 24:6- For by wise counsel thou shalt make thy war: and in the multitude of counselors there is safety. King Solomon, the wisest and richest King in the history of mankind instructs us through the wisdom of God that it is only by wise counsel and spiritual direction are told to make our war- which is the war of this life, the struggles, the challenges we face daily and the arrows of darkness been thrown to us by the devil and his agents.The scripture says that in the multitude of counselors there is safety.A counselor is someone who is given the foresight or foreknowledge of a situation and he is capable through his advice and consultation to bring solution to that which is brought forth. The greatest Counselor any man can have is the HOLY SPIRIT: HE IS THE AUTHOR OF THE WORD. The Bible says that all scriptures are inspired by the Breath of God and the Breath of God is the Spirit.It is imperative therefore as Christians and believers to rely on the word of God and the Holy Spirit as the COUNSELORS OF OUR LIFE. The Bible teaches us that without counsel we will not be able to stand the test of time. Proverbs 11:14- Where no counsel is, the people fall: but in the multitude of counselors there is safety.

Great men and women of God who accomplished extraordinary things in their life always inquire from the LORD who spoke in His word by the mouths and writings of the prophets and apostles. The scriptures says one of David's counselors had the spirit of wisdom that the counsels or advice he gave was as if a man had inquired from the oracle of God.

'And the counsel of Ahithophel, which he counselled in those days, was as if a man had enquired at the oracle of God: so was all the counsel of Ahithophel both with David and with Absalom' (2nd Samuel 16:23)

The oracle of God represents the mouth piece of God and out of the mouth piece of God is the Holy Scriptures birthed.

ENTERING INTO THE PROPHETIC REALMS
OF THE PSALMS

As you become obedient to the spiritual counsel given by the Holy Spirit through His word in the psalms, you will encounter greater power and you will deepen your relationship with God spoke through David His servant. According to Jewish folklore, it is said that whenever the HOLY SPIRIT came upon King David, he took his musical instrument and began to write and play his songs out unto God. It was spirit to Spirit communication, the birthplace of divine miracles.

Psalm 1(aleph) : This psalm must be prayed when you are in the greatest need and also powerful against the spirit of bareness and potential miscarriage. Using low tone voice and earnest prayer, meditate deeply upon this psalm trusting in the power of God to establish that which you have laid before Him.

Write your request below:

Psalm 2 (bet) – Pray this scripture when you are surrounded by enemies both visible and invisible and the rulers that gather together against you shall be put into confusion. It is suitable if you have fear of untimely death and accident

Psalm 3 (Gimmel) - when you are overwhelmed and troubled by the affairs of life and you cannot establish your destiny, cry unto God using this psalm for 7(seven day) and the light of God will shine through your destiny in Jesus name.

Psalm 4 (Dalet)- Pray this prayer when you are in need and seek favor before God and men, the God of grace, merciful and loving God will dispose the heart of men towards you. Pray this psalm at dawn or early in the morning with strong faith in God and you will have your desire

Psalm 5 (Hey)- Pray this psalm when you need favor from God or men, pray this psalm 7 times daily and you shall surely receive favor in your endeavors.

Psalm 6 (Vav) - Pray this psalm when you are sick and you need healing from God. Pray the psalm over olive oil and anoint yourself, you can also pray over a cup of water and drink it. It is also good for healing eye problems.

Psalm 7 (Zayin) - Prayer against enemies at work place or whenever you find yourself in a strange environment and you become fearful of their activities. Praying this psalm daily will put fear in your enemies and they will not be able to do you harm

Psalm 8 (Chet) - Vengeance upon your enemies. God through this psalm will empower your tongue that you will overcome your enemies through prayer and the power of your words. If you seek to receive authority against demons through your words, recite this psalm and by the name of Jesus, you will conquer all evil spirits.

Psalm 9 (Tet)- when your child becomes sick or ails, pray this psalm over a cup of water and trusting in the healing power of Jesus,anoint your child with the water and you will see the healing grace of Our Lord Jesus Christ

Psalm 10 (Yod)- Pray this psalm if you have been oppressed, and depressed by demonic activity in your life, or in any form of addiction-smoking, alcohol, sex...pray this psalm in the name of Jesus over an olive oil and anoint yourself breaking free from every demonic hold over your life in Jesus name.

Psalm 11(Yud aleph) - Pray this psalm if you experience demonic traps/confinement and delays. Trust in the deliverance power of the Holy Spirit, get an olive oil, and pray the psalm. After the prayer break the olive oil with the bottle and you will be set free in Jesus name.

Psalm 12(Yud bet) - Daily reading of this psalm will cause you to experience favor

Psalm 13 (yud-gimmel)- if you have been unsuccessful in establishing a business- pray this psalm daily and God will give you ideas in dreams and in thoughts for your business to flourish

Psalm 14 (Yud Dalet)- Using this psalm, bind every demonic activity and the work of the enemy against your life, the fool says in his heart, there is no God, let every foolish activity of the enemy in your life be destroyed in the name of Jesus.

Psalm 15 (tet vav)- Pray this psalm if you want power in your tongue to perform miracles in Jesus name, pray for 7 nights and you will anoint your tongue with honey and olive oil and you will command all forces by the power of the Holy Spirit in Jesus name.

COMBINATION/MATRIX OF THE PSALMS

Psalm 29 (caf –tet) Read this psalm over a cup of water before you sleep and wash your face before you sleep, trusting the Lord of dreams to give you a revelation concerning your life. This psalm is also powerful in casting demons.

Psalm 31 (Lamed alef)- Pray this psalm at midnight against the evil eye .Every monitoring spirit against your life will be destroyed by the power of Jesus Christ

Psalm 49 (mem tet) Pray this psalm over a cup of water if you are sick or you have fever, drink the water after prayers and trusting the healing power of Jesus, you will be healed instantly

Psalm 67 (samech zayin) - if you find yourself in demonic imprisonment/physical confinement or if your loved one is in prison: pray this psalm fervently daily and the Lord God will show mercy and deliverance

Psalm 91 (tsadik alef) - pray this psalm fervently against illness and demons. No demonic power will be able to withstand this psalm. Pray at midnight.

Psalm 109 (Kuf Tet)-Pray this psalm over olive oil or water and anoint yourself twice if you find yourself troubled by evil dreams and night mares. Trusting in the great power of God, you will overcome all powers of evil in Jesus name.

Psalm 121 (Kuf chaf alef)-Pray this psalm if you experience evil dreams/ threats and night mares. The good angels of God will visit in your dream daily if you pray fervently trusting in the power of God

Psalm 28 (caf-chet) - pray this psalm daily for marital breakthrough and against poverty

Psalm 30 (Lamed) - Pray this psalm against illness

Psalm 64 (samech dalet) - Pray this psalm daily against accidents and enemies

Psalm 94 (tsadik dalet) - Against demonic curses/hexes and spells

Psalm 65 (samech hey) – Pray this psalm for good fortune, abundance and prosperity

Psalm 111 (kuf yud alef) - Pray this psalm to strengthen deep love and relationship bonds between couples

Psalm 129 (kuf chaf tet) - Pray this psalm against demonic oppression

Psalm 113 (kuf yud gimmel)- If you are barren and experiencing difficulty in child birth, pray this psalm over an olive oil and anoint your belly daily and God will open the door of your womb and bless you with children in Jesus name

Psalm 20, 34, and 119:41-48- Pray this psalm in the same order as shown here and you will have open doors and promotion in Jesus name.

For pregnant women- if you want your children to be beautiful when they are born, pray **Ezekiel 16:13** every night before the birth of your child and that which is written in the word shall be unto your child

Psalm 47 (mem zayin) - Use this psalm to pray for healing

Psalm 13, 26, 27, 28 108 and 105- Using the combination of these psalms to pray over an olive oil daily and anointing yourself will attract the blessings and success of God upon your business.

Psalm 81 (Pei alef) - pray this psalm if you are looking for a new job or change of employment. Pray fervently at midnight and trusting God to give you grace

Psalm 22 (caf bet)- if you are suffering from alcoholic addiction, pray this psalm daily over a cup of water and mix it with olive oil and drink it and the power of addiction will be broken in Jesus name.

Psalm 127 (kuf chaf zayin) –Success for children- parents should pray this psalm daily over their children and they will become successful people in life in Jesus name.

Psalm 110 (kuf yud) – pray this psalm if you are plagued with shyness and low self-esteem, trust in the Lord and He will give you confidence

Psalm 11, 4, and 20- Pray this psalm if you find yourself in the court of law, pray to the JUDGE of the WORLD and he will show mercy and give you a favorable verdict

Psalm 116 (kuf tet zayin)- Praying this psalm fervently will override every spirit of death in Jesus mighty name.

Psalm 108 (kuf chet) – Pray this psalm if you have been abandoned and face spousal rejection, trust the Lord and he will cause a change in your life and give you comfort.

Psalm 13, 31, and 87 – Pray this psalm daily and fervently if you are suffering from depression and God will redeem you

Psalm 41 (mem alef)- Hospital admission- if you or a loved one is sick in the hospital, pray this psalm fervently and the Lord will raise the sick out of bed in Jesus name.

Psalm 91, 32, and 69- Pray this psalm for protection and safety

Psalm 66 (samech vav) Pray this psalm for increased faith

Psalm 133 (kuf lamed gimmel) - Pray this psalm for harmony among family

Psalm 78, 145 – for supply and abundance of food

Psalm 44 (mem dalet) – use this psalm for forgiveness

Psalm 143 (kuf mem gimmel) pray this psalm daily for good news

Psalm 37 (lamed zayin) pray this psalm for good publicity

Psalm 12- for protection against gossip

Psalm 117, 150 – Thanksgiving

Psalm 11, 39, 43, 49 and 119- Guidance through dreams and visions, pray these psalms nightly before you sleep

Psalm 144 (kuf mem dalet) - Pray this psalm to be skilful in the use of your hands

Psalm 71 (ayin alef) - Pray this psalm for happiness in old age

Psalm 44, 45- pray these psalms for marital harmony

Psalm 67, 92- pray these psalms for good health

Psalm 93, 122- Blessing of a house

Psalm 9, 33- pray these psalms fervently over olive oil and water and anoint yourself if you suffer from impotence

Psalm 99 (tsadik tet) - Pray this psalm for divine inspiration to write a book or a song, pray daily and at midnight and the Lord will inspire you

Psalm 90, 119, and 128 – Pray these psalms daily for long life

Psalm 110. 111- Pray these psalms to be likeable and influential

Psalms 52, 72, 106 and 108 – for prosperity

Psalm 19 (Yud taf) - Public speaking – pray this psalm before your speech and you will be received gracefully in Jesus name.

Ezekiel 16:6- Pray this prayer if you are wounded and fear death.

Psalm 6, 129- Pray over olive oil and anoint affected area to relieve pain.

90 DAYS CHALLENGE THROUGH THE BOOK OF PSALMS

I encourage you dear reader and beloved child of God to take the opportunity to read the entire book of psalms within 90 days which is a period of 3 months.

There are 150 psalms in the Holy Scriptures, please read 50 psalms every month starting from the first psalm to the end. I promise you by the power of the Holy Spirit that you will encounter divine blessings and your relationship with God will deepen in Jesus name.

90 Days Challenge TRACKER

Mina and Her Blog.com

My New Habit:...
Started : ....
Completed on:...

1	2	3	4	5	6	7	8	9	10	11	12	13	14	15	16	17
18	19	20	21	22	23	24	25	26	27	28	29	30	31	32	33	34
35	36	37	38	39	40	41	42	43	44	45	46	47	48	49	50	51
52	53	54	55	56	57	58	59	60	61	62	63	64	65	66	67	68
69	70	71	72	73	74	75	76	77	78	79	80	81	82	83	84	85
86	87	88	89	90												

90 Days Challenge Tracker Printable

END NOTE

http:home.iae.nl/users/lightnet/creator/jesusmyth6.htm

English Translation of the cathechism of the Catholic Church for the United States of America (1997).United states catholic conference, Inc

Tree of Life- Israel Regardie

For Dangerous Prayers –Power Through the Psalms

Please contact: Apostle Dennis Adjei –Sarpong

www.holyghostfirenow.com

3250 Perry ave apt 6j

Bronx, New York, 10467

Tel: 3472575296

Emai:healing@holyghostfirenow.com

Made in the USA
Middletown, DE
23 September 2022